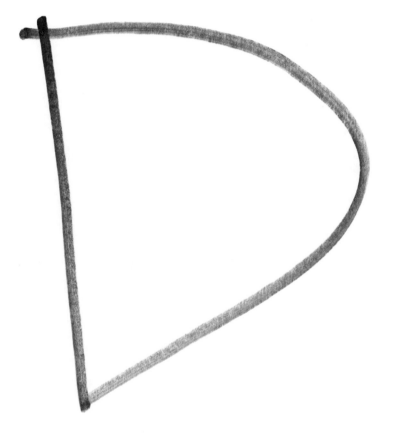

What
Do You
Mean
I Have
a Learning
Disability?

What Do You Mean
I Have a Learning Disability?

KATHLEEN M. DWYER

PHOTOGRAPHS BY BARBARA BEIRNE

Walker and Company New York

First published in the United States of America in 1991
by Walker Publishing Company, Inc.

Published simultaneously in Canada by Thomas Allen & Son
Canada, Limited, Markham, Ontario

Library of Congress Cataloging-in-Publication Data
Dwyer, Kathleen Marie, 1951–
What do you mean I have a learning disability? / by Kathleen M.
Dwyer; photographs by Barbara Beirne.
p.   cm.
Summary: Describes learning disabilities and what can be done to
overcome them.
ISBN 0-8027-8103-9 (reinforced) — ISBN 0-8027-8102-0
1. Learning disabilities—United States—Juvenile literature.
[1. Learning disabilities.] I. Beirne, Barbara, ill. II. Title.
LC4705.W53   1991
371.9—dc20   90-29155
CIP
AC

Printed in the United States of America

2   4   6   8   10   9   7   5   3   1

This book is dedicated to two wonderful sons,
Jay Beirne
and
Kevin Marshall Dwyer

We would like to thank Jimmy and his family, as well as all the
children and teachers who made this project so enjoyable.

Jimmy is ten years old. He has two brothers, Daniel and Peter. They all live with their parents in a small town near a big city. Jimmy is happiest when he is running as fast as he can.

People say Jimmy is shy, and he does try to get by without too many people noticing him. He thinks it's easier to be quiet than to be noticed. He loves his Mom and Dad, and he knows they love him. They understand when he is having one of his quiet times.

Jimmy loves it when his Mom and Dad look in the family photo album and tell stories about him and his two brothers when they were little. Once, when he was three years old, he climbed up and took Daddy's screwdriver from the workbench. He took the screwdriver to the bathroom door and unscrewed the bottom hinge. Mommy tells about how she went to open the door and it almost fell off. She pretends that she had been really upset, but he knows that she tells him this story because it makes him laugh and because she thought he was smart.

He doesn't try to take things apart or put them together much anymore. He thinks other kids can do things better.

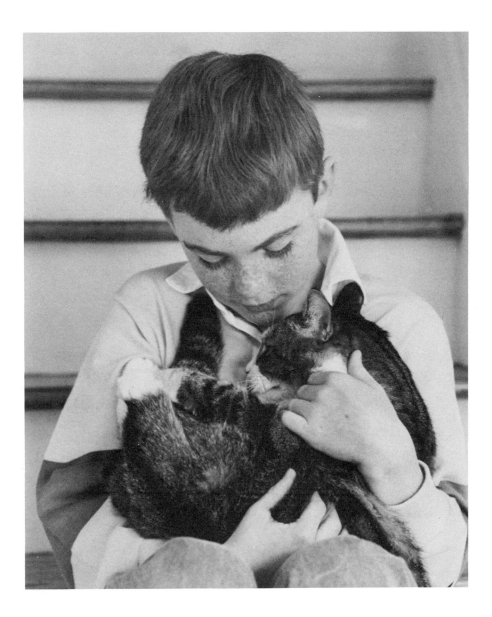

Jimmy has a secret. One day he whispers to his cat, Ebenezer, "I'm so stupid. I know I am." It feels good to tell somebody. He is glad Ebenezer can keep a secret too.

Jimmy loves working outside with his dad. One day when he is feeling down, he tells Dad about his secret. He says, "I'm just dumb." Dad tries to cheer him up. He says, "Of course you're not dumb. You're smart; all my boys are smart."

Jimmy thinks his two older brothers are as smart as anything. He's sure they will go to college and be famous someday. Jimmy loves hanging out in his brothers' rooms, but some of the time they think he is a pest and they tell him to "bug off."

*H*ow can he be smart when he is always losing things? Mornings seem to be hurrying time because no matter how early he gets up, he always loses time looking for something. He can't even find the right shoes in the morning. His mom has to run after him because he goes off to school without his lunch. Jimmy really can't understand why he does that because he is hungry all the time and he would never miss lunch on purpose. He forgets to bring the right books home to study for tests. Actually, this isn't so bad. Teachers can't say he is dumb for not knowing the answers. They just yell at him for forgetting to take his books home.

Jimmy never knows how his words will come out.

"Oops, I said 'pisgetti' again."

*L*ots of times people giggle when his words get mixed up. He often speaks very quietly so that he will not make great, loud mistakes. Most of the time that works because people leave him alone when he is quiet. He just smiles, but inside he feels bad.

*N*o wonder when he thinks about school he wishes he could just stay in bed in the mornings, but his mom keeps making him get up. Sometimes, he thinks that when he grows up he will live in the woods with the animals. It really would be easier than reading and working with a whole lot of papers.

20% F

Jimmy
Science

1 *eromobanes* X *sp*

2 *mpgoats* X *sp*

3 *nukles* X *sp*

4 *mightacodra* *sp*

5 *Crotplcation* *sp*

6 *sidaptation* X *sp*

7 *ovem* X

8 *ovules*

9 *stamen*

the main parts of a leaf are X

He wonders why his letters get all mixed up. That never seems
to happen to anyone else. He hates it when the teacher puts "SP"
all over his paper. He hates being told he makes careless errors.
He is really trying so hard.

When he does a math problem at the board, he feels every single kid is laughing at him. He thinks he is doing it right and out comes the wrong answer. Still, this isn't nearly as bad as being called upon to read out loud in front of the whole class. That makes him more scared than anything.

Jimmy is always in trouble. You would think he was doing things on purpose the way everyone keeps telling him,

"Jimmy, sit in your seat."

"Jimmy, why don't you pay attention? You've lost your place again."

"Jimmy, don't tell me you left your homework at home again."

"Go back to your seat. I explained that already."

Some days he feels the only teacher who doesn't yell at him is the librarian.

om is Jimmy's very best friend, and he doesn't mind when Jimmy does dumb things. They share their secrets, their good times, and their treasures. They are good to each other. Tom doesn't make fun of Jimmy when he gets mixed up, and somehow Jimmy never gets embarrassed in front of Tom.

They know what it means to have a true best friend.

*H*is mother and father often talk about Jimmy. "Do you notice how Jimmy gets upset when he can't do his homework?" asks Mom.

"I've been worried about him since we found out he has been fighting in school. That just isn't like our Jimmy," replies Dad.

"When we got those late papers to be signed, and the failed test papers, I started to get *very* worried. As the work gets harder in school he seems to be falling further and further behind. He tries so many things to avoid doing his homework. What are we going to do for him?" Mom sighs.

Conference time always makes Jimmy's mother nervous. She expects to be told "Jimmy is just not trying." This year is different.

Mrs. Brown, Jimmy's homeroom teacher, tells his mother, "I know Jimmy is smart, but I think there is something holding him back. I think he should be tested."

After the conference, Jimmy's mother and father sit down with him and tell him that they think he should be tested. That sounds like a terrible idea to Jimmy. He hates taking tests.

One good thing about testing is that he gets to take the day off from school, but that doesn't help much. He still has a terrible feeling in the pit of his stomach.

Jimmy and his mom go to meet Dr. Stone. When Dr. Stone greets him and asks how he is, Jimmy lies and says, "I'm fine, thank you."

She seems "OK" for a tester, if you have to have one.

Jimmy has two long sessions of testing. It doesn't start out too badly. Dr. Stone seems to be doing most of the work. Jimmy just answers some questions and moves some blocks and puzzles around.

It does seem different than that stupid testing they do in school. Dr. Stone smiles a lot, and after a while Jimmy starts to think it's not so bad after all. He does end up doing tests on spelling, reading, and math, but at least no other kids are watching.

*A*fter the testing is all over, Mom and Dad and Jimmy have a conference with Dr. Stone. His parents seem to be happy when Dr. Stone tells them that she did find something out from Jimmy's testing. There is a reason that he is failing in school. He has a learning disability.

Jimmy is confused. His parents seem happy, but he isn't sure what is going on. "What do you mean I have a learning disability?" asks Jimmy.

*D*r. Stone says, "Well, Jimmy, a child or an adult with a learning disability is one with average or above average intelligence who has trouble learning certain skills like speaking, reading, writing, spelling, or math."

Jimmy says, "I don't know what that means."

Dr. Stone replies, "Did you ever look in the mirror and get mixed up on which way your hand was doing something?"

"Yes," says Jimmy, "that happened to me just the other day when Mom told me to part my hair. I kept going the wrong way."

"Well, that's kind of what happens when you have a learning disability. Your brain plays tricks on you when you look at letters and numbers. They come out all wrong sometimes. The interesting thing is that you can be really smart and have this happen to you. I understand how difficult it is for you to have a learning disability, but the nice thing about it is that it can be fixed," says Dr. Stone.

"Are you sure I'm not just stupid?" asks Jimmy.

"Not at all, Jimmy. Let me explain," says Dr. Stone.

"You really can learn, but you have to be taught in a different way. There are some wonderful teachers who can help children with learning disabilities. The children do very well once they get this special kind of teaching. You are very smart, Jimmy, and I know that a special teacher will help you very much," explains Dr. Stone.

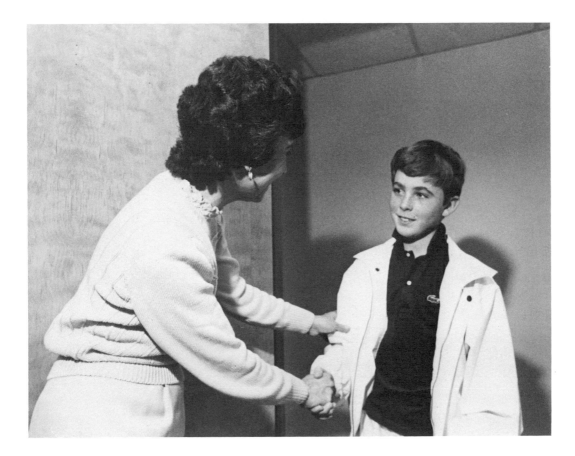

Jimmy is referred to a tutor, Mrs. Sanchez, for help with his learning disability. Mrs. Sanchez makes him feel better because she understands why he makes mistakes. She tells him she will help make school easier for him.

*H*e finds out he isn't the only one going to see Mrs. Sanchez. There are other kids who are smart and have the same problems.

Mrs. Sanchez and Jimmy start with the alphabet. Jimmy gets some of the sounds mixed up, so he has to learn key words to go with each letter or group of letters. It seems silly at first, but in a little while he is getting the sounds right most of the time. He learns how to break words into syllables and how to put syllables together to read words.

Mrs. Sanchez says that some of the work is in visual perception, which is what his brain tells him he sees. He is learning why his eyes play tricks on him and make him reverse his letters and numbers.

They do rhythmic writing at the blackboard.

They work with blocks and numbers

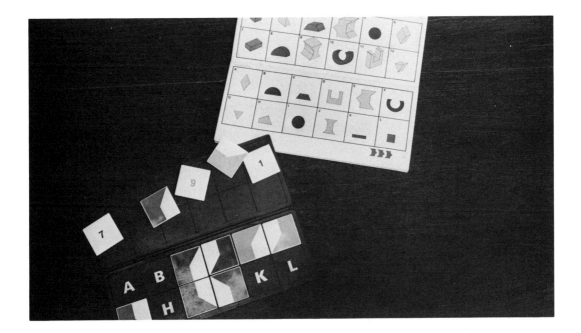

and all sorts of interesting puzzles and games.

*A*fter a while Jimmy notices that his schoolwork doesn't take him as long. He is finishing his work in class as fast as the other kids. He is finishing his homework in much less time, too. When he reads things, he is starting to know what some of it says. He doesn't seem to reverse his letters as much anymore. Jimmy is working harder, but things seem to be going better. He isn't making all those mistakes, and when he makes one, he usually finds it himself.

He still has to take those dumb old tests, and he still hates them. Every time he takes one that awful feeling in his stomach comes back.

One day he takes this really hard Social Studies test. He did study for it, and he remembers what some of the words on the test mean, but he is sure he will get his usual "D." He remembers what his mom always tells him, "Just do the best you can, Jimmy."

After the test, the teacher hands back the test papers. Jimmy is prepared to take his paper and just shove it into his desk as he usually does. He keeps listening for his name. Finally, his teacher says, "Here is a paper I am very proud of. I know the hard work that went into it. Congratulations, Jimmy. You got an 'A'!"

★ A Jimmy

Social Studies

1. Fort Sumter

2. Confederate and Union

3. Abraham Lincoln

4. Blockade

5. Gettysburg

6. One of the major battles of the Civil War was the battle of Vicksburg. The fleet ran past the city's guns at night. General Grant moved in from the south to capture the city.

Jimmy can't wait to run home from school that day. He is so excited. He runs into the house and yells, "Guess what, Mom, I got an 'A'!"

Mom gives him a big kiss. Everyone is happy for him. Even his brothers, Peter and Daniel, tease him about being the smartest one in the family now.

Jimmy knows he still has a lot of hard work ahead of him, but now he is starting to think he is smart after all. It's a really neat feeling.

One day his teacher asks everyone to write a paragraph about "feelings." Jimmy knows just what to write.

Jimmy

It is wonderful to get an "A" To know that I am smart is a wonderful feeling. I know that I'm just as good as everyone else. Now I know I am just as good as my brothers. I'm not sad all the time about bad grades. I know that I won't be stupid when I grow up.

Other People with Learning Disabilities

Hans Christian Andersen
Joyce Bulifant
Stephen Cannell
Cher
Agatha Christie
Tom Cruise
Leonardo da Vinci
Thomas Edison
Albert Einstein
Margaux Hemingway
Bruce Jenner
Greg Luganis
Steve McQueen
David Murdock
Lucy Baines Johnson Nugent
Nelson Rockefeller
Rodin
Jackie Stewart
Lindsey Wagner
Woodrow Wilson
Henry Winkler

Sources of Help

AMERICAN PSYCHOLOGICAL ASSOCIATION
1200 Seventeenth Street N.W.
Washington, DC 20036
(202) 833-7600

ASSOCIATION FOR CHILDREN AND ADULTS WITH LEARNING DISABILITIES
4156 Library Road
Pittsburgh, PA 15234
(412) 341-1515

FOUNDATION FOR CHILDREN WITH LEARNING DISABILITIES
99 Park Avenue
New York, NY 10016
(212) 687-7211

NATIONAL INSTITUTE OF CHILD HEALTH AND HUMAN DEVELOPMENT
National Institutes of Health,
U.S. Department of Health and Human Services
Building 31
Bethesda, MD 20205
(301) 496-5133

THE ORTON DYSLEXIA SOCIETY
8415 Bellona Lane
Towson, MD 21204
(301) 296-0232

NATIONAL INSTITUTE FOR LEARNING DISABILITIES
107 Seekel Street
Norfolk, VA 23505
(804) 423-8646